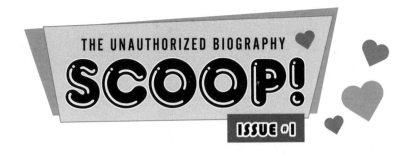

THE UNAUTHORIZED BIOGRAPHY

SCOOP!

ISSUE #1

Noah Centineo

by C. H. Mitford

D0612613

Grosset & Dunlap

GROSSET & DUNLAP
An Imprint of Penguin Random House LLC, New York

If you purchased this book without a cover, you should be aware that this book is stolen property. It was reported as "unsold and destroyed" to the publisher, and neither the author nor the publisher has received any payment for this "stripped book."

Penguin supports copyright. Copyright fuels creativity, encourages diverse voices, promotes free speech, and creates a vibrant culture. Thank you for buying an authorized edition of this book and for complying with copyright laws by not reproducing, scanning, or distributing any part of it in any form without permission. You are supporting writers and allowing Penguin to continue to publish books for every reader.

The publisher does not have any control over and does not assume any responsibility for author or third-party websites or their content.

Illustrations by Becky James

Photo credit: cover: Matt Winkelmeyer/Staff/Getty Images Entertainment/ Getty Images North America

Copyright © 2020 by Penguin Random House LLC. All rights reserved. Published by Grosset & Dunlap, an imprint of Penguin Random House LLC, New York. GROSSET & DUNLAP is a registered trademark of Penguin Random House LLC. Printed in the USA.

Visit us online at www.penguinrandomhouse.com.

ISBN 9780593222256   10 9 8 7 6 5 4 3 2 1

TABLE OF CONTENTS

CHAPTER 1

TO ALL THE WORK I'VE DONE BEFORE

When you think of Noah Centineo, you probably think of the superstar who won the 2019 MTV Best Breakthrough Performance Award for playing Peter Kavinsky in *To All the Boys I've Loved Before*. Totally deserved, right? I mean, nothing is cuter than that hand in the back pocket. And Noah is the epitome of charm with that hot tub splash and his love of Kitty's Korean yogurts.

> But here's the **SCOOP!** Noah has been honing his acting chops for over a DECADE. From the outside, it looks like a rapid rise—literally shooting to stardom—but we know better, don't we?

Back in 2009, when he was just thirteen, Noah started out in the film *The Gold Retrievers* as Josh Peters, who saves the family from losing both their home and their beloved golden retriever, Bosco, by finding a long-lost treasure and fighting criminals and rabid bears along the way. Noah was as cute as the puppy!

Then there were bit parts in two Disney TV series, *Austin & Ally* and *Shake It Up.* Next was the part of Jaden Stark in 2014's *How to Build a Better Boy* (perfect title for him!), followed by joining the cast of another Disney pilot called *Growing Up and Down*, which was initially not picked up. So, he wasn't exactly coming out of the gate winning Oscars.

Noah C.—or NC, as we like to call him—went through a truly rough time. Because he'd signed a contract for the pilot, he couldn't take jobs during that time period, even though the show didn't come to fruition. He explained to MTV News that, "I went through a really dark patch because I wasn't actually allowed to work. I was contractually obligated to be on hold for a certain amount of months. And that sucked miserably."

But NC was not to be daunted! He kept at his craft, and, man, did it pay off. He auditioned exhaustively, taking some small roles until he landed the role of Jesus Adams Foster in *The Fosters*. Here's where things turned around for Noah! This is a very moving series, and Noah lends both gravitas and charisma to a character who is warm and loyal but also struggling with ADHD.

So, from there, BAM! Noah was cast in another series, *T@gged*, a creepy thriller. He plays—you guessed it!—the boyfriend, Hawk Carter. Do you sense a pattern here? From there, he progressed to heartthrob surfer Johnny Sanders Jr. in *SPF-18* and, lo and behold, one of the first of many times Noah is shirtless on film. The movie didn't get great reviews, but nothing was going to stop him now. He branched out into the supernatural for the movie *Can't Take It Back,* which prompted

Dread Central writer Jonathan Barkan to write the headline "Exclusive: *Can't Take It Back* Clip Proves My Fear of Pencils Correct." While these weren't blockbusters, they got Noah on a streak. And we know where that led him! *Sierra Burgess Is a Loser* is where it led him. And what a lead!

And here's another SCOOP! Noah almost wasn't cast as Jamey! He didn't even audition for that role; he tried out for the part of Spence, the rude guy who dates the popular girl.

Sweet, likable Noah as Spence? No way! Director Ian Samuels thought about the casting process very thoroughly, and he didn't want the Jamey character to be too obvious. Not the usual in-your-face, handsome-but-vapid jock. "With Jamey, we were looking for somebody who could play a more soulful type and somebody with the puppy-dog eyes who the girls would like," Samuels explained to *ET*. "But who . . . kind of had a unique sincerity to him, and Noah absolutely did. It was kind of crazy, honestly."

Soulful is right. It's a rare quality in a young actor who is also drop-dead gorgeous. And Noah Centineo has soul in spades. It's the only way we could believe Brooks Rattigan's transition from a striving dreamer who gets caught up in the big hustle of his gigolo-but-not-dating service and the lure of Ivy and Big Leagues to ultimately becoming an empathetic son, friend, and boyfriend after his AHA! moment, realizing that if you have to fake it, it's not worth making it. For reals. Not the plus-one dating service kind. And it's the only way we could believe that lacrosse star Peter could simultaneously pine after the popular diva and gradually, and oh-so-sweetly, fall for the smart, cool, kind (and adorable!) Lara Jean.

Double SCOOP! It turns out that Centineo is so talented, lots of Kavinsky's charm came from his own improv!

9

Remember the sweet pillow fight with Lara Jean's sister, Kitty, where he saves the bowl by moving it out of the way before the feathers fly? Totally Noah's move.

"Noah improvising that moment means that not only is his character a spatially aware king, but that Noah is one himself! That's one step closer to the twenty-two-year-old actor literally being the Peter Kavinsky of everyone's dreams," says *Mashable*.

So, Centineo has acting chops and charm for sure. And even though the MTV Best Breakthrough Performance Award makes it seem like he came out of nowhere, he told *The Hollywood Reporter* that, "The following is overnight. The career is not." Clearly, he plans to stick around awhile.

*N*ow that you're an expert on Noah's filmography, can you guess which of his characters said the following lines?

↓ TAKE THIS QUIZ TO TEST ↓ YOUR KNOWLEDGE!

1 "For the record, I think roses are the b**chy supermodels of flowers."

A. Jaden Stark
B. Jamey
C. Brooks Rattigan
D. Hawk Carter

A. Brooks Rattigan
B. Jaden Stark
C. Peter Kavinsky
D. Johnny Sanders Jr.

2 "You know, people usually check behind them before they reverse to avoid killing others . . . It's a thing we do."

3

"But through it all there were little pockets of air when I felt like I was truly myself, and that was when I was with you."

A. Jamey
B. Jesus Adams Foster
C. Brooks Rattigan
D. Hawk Carter

A. Jamey
B. Jake Roberts
C. Hawk Carter
D. Jesus Adams Foster

4

"Excuse me, my buddy wants your phone number because he wants to know the best way to get ahold of me in the morning."

5

"Salt air is magic like that."

A. Johnny Sanders Jr.
B. Peter Kavinsky
C. Jesus Adams Foster
D. Hawk Carter

6

"You have the references of an eighty-year-old woman."

A. Jesus Adams Foster
B. Peter Kavinsky
C. Jaden Stark
D. Jamey

A. Jaden Stark
B. Peter Kavinsky
C. Brooks Rattigan
D. Johnny Sanders Jr.

7

"You want to save me a cookie?"

8

"There is nothing anyone can say to change the way I feel about my family."

A. Jesus Adams Foster
B. Johnny Sanders Jr.
C. Jamey
D. Hawk Carter

How did you do? Check your answers on page 95.

0–3 correct: Keep reading!

4–6 correct: You're getting there!

7–8 correct: You're a Centineo superfan!

We're so excited about what comes next for Noah (more on that later!). But first . . .

let's take a quick step back . . .

CHAPTER 2

ALL IN THE FAMILY

SO WE'RE GUESSING YOU KNOW THE DEETS:

NAME: Noah Gregory Centineo

BIRTHPLACE: Miami, Florida

BIRTHDATE: May 9, 1996

HEIGHT: 6'1"

PARENTS: Kellee Janel and Gregory Vincent Centineo

SIBLING: Taylor Centineo

These seem like pretty simple facts, but they can tell us a lot about Noah!

First of all, the cool last name: Centineo. Noah says, "I'm Italian, Native American. I believe I have a bit of Puerto Rican in me, and I'm Dutch." One of the many things we love about the name Centineo is that in Italian, *cento* means one hundred. Like, 100 percent. Doesn't this totally fit? The dude is all about 100 percent. We know how hard he worked to jump-start his career, and we know he never gives up. If you want big things, you have to give 100 percent for your dream. It seems as though Noah Centineo, like his name, was born knowing that.

After a lot of false starts, we now know how to pronounce it, too, thanks to *Teen Vogue*: "It's not 'Cen-TIN-ee-oh. It's softer, more relaxed, like a slow wave across a smooth-pebbled coastline, like brushing a curly lock of deep brown hair off of a forehead—'Cen-tin-AYE-oh.'"

He probably gets a lot of his sense of fun from his birthplace, Miami. That easy southern vibe came from somewhere! And *The Perfect Date* was filmed in New Orleans. I think we're starting to see a pattern . . .

SCOOP! FACTS
ON MIAMI, FLORIDA

Did you know that Miami is the only major US city that was founded by a woman?

THAT'S RIGHT! Julia Tuttle, a local businesswoman, encouraged a developer to extend a railroad to Miami, which would soon lead to the development of modern Miami.

Did you know that Miami gets its name from a Native tribe, the Mayaimi, who once lived there?

Here's another SCOOP! for you: In their native language, *mayaimi* meant "big water." The Mayaimi lived by Lake Mayaimi, which is now Lake Okeechobee.

May 9 places Noah squarely as a Taurus. We already knew that whoever dates Noah is lucky, duh! But check this out: Those born under this astrological sign are loyal and trustworthy. They prefer monogamy over dating around (we're looking at you, Kavinsky). Tauruses want to spoil and protect their significant others, as well as lavish them with gifts. Hmmm . . . like love notes?

Does it get any better than this? There must be a catch.

Well, there are always two sides to every coin, and a lot of people hear Taurus the bull and think "stubborn." But it seems to us that the stubborn side of Noah aligns more with his stick-to-it vibe regarding his career. You don't get far in the cutthroat entertainment industry without being very, *very* determined.

Plus, the Taurus is affectionate and gentle and always, always is thinking of family. Which brings me to the rest of the Centineos! They are incredibly supportive of Noah and his career.

If it weren't for his sister, Taylor, he wouldn't have a career at all. He was dragged along on her modeling auditions. One day, someone saw him, and BOOM! Noah told *Esquire* magazine, "I'm like an eight-year-old, and someone told me they could make me a star, and my eyes got real big." Not surprising that he would get spotted, and fast!

Isn't it crazy to think that it almost never happened at all?

"There's an alternate universe out there where an eight-year-old Centineo was never forced to [tag] along with his older sister, Taylor, to an open casting call at a South Florida talent agency as she pursued her dream of being a model and, in turn, was never encouraged to audition himself," *E! News* said.

The family is *full-on* about creativity. Noah's dad, Gregory Vincent Centineo, is an executive producer for film, plus they brought him to many auditions and commercials. Noah got into BAK Middle School of the Arts, an A-rated school where they inspire excellence in both the arts and academics. Sounds like that 100 percent again!

Noah never fails to be a gentleman and give back, so of course he thanked BAK during his acceptance of the 2019 Nickelodeon Kids' Choice award for Favorite Movie Actor. His kindness didn't go unnoticed, and BAK wrote back, "We are so proud of you . . . To hear you SHOUT OUT to Bak MSOA was AWESOME! Thank you for supporting #ArtsEducation."

Are you wondering where he got that huge dose of kindness and consideration? Well, we know a large part of it comes from the Centineo family.

Plus, more SCOOP! His mom, Kellee, even moved with him to Los Angeles to further his odds at stardom. WHOA! I mean, lots of parents can't even be persuaded to go shopping down the street, much less move across the country to chase a dream!

Even after arriving in LA, it didn't immediately happen. Jobs were at times dicey, especially when he had that forced contractual downtime after

Growing Up and Down wasn't picked up.

Like any sane parents, Noah's told him to get a job and go to college. "So I got a job and I enrolled in college, but I was begging them, 'Please, just give me the summer, give me the summer.'"

Noah put in 100 percent, and it led to a windfall: the part of Jesus Adams Foster in *The Fosters*. Phew! But clearly the guy is meant to be on camera, so he had good odds. And an even better family support system!

Since we're all about where we come from in this chap, here's a list of the top ten coolest locations where Noah has filmed . . .

SCOOP! EXTRA

LOCATION, LOCATION, LOCATION

10 Albuquerque, New Mexico, for *T@gged*

9 Los Angeles, California, for *Sierra Burgess Is a Loser*

8 Fort Langley, British Columbia, Canada, for *To All the Boys: P.S. I Still Love You*

7 Palm Beach County, Florida, for *Swiped*

6 Vancouver, Canada, for *To All the Boys I've Loved Before*

5 Prague, Czech Republic, for *The Diary*

4 Shanghai, China, for *The Diary*

3 Berlin, Germany, for *Charlie's Angels (2019)*

2 Malibu, California, for *SPF-18*

1 New Orleans, Louisiana, for *The Perfect Date*

PS: We just gave you the SCOOP! on what's coming up for Noah! Did you see it? More details in CHAPTER 7: WHAT'S NEXT?

CHAPTER 3

FRIENDS AND MORE THAN FRIENDS

So, there's Lara Jean . . . and I, oops, we mean Lana. Wait. No, actually, we don't! We won't blame you for shipping Peter and LJ because Noah and Lana made you *believe* in their connection. And if you felt it wasn't just acting, you weren't wrong.

The SCOOP! is that they had intense chemistry. So intense, in fact, that they had to do something about it!

They hung out together before filming, and Lana said, "We had just come back from a hot yoga class and we went to his apartment, and we ordered pizza, and it's kind of, like, like, ooh, hot yoga, pizza, what's happening? It was right before we shot the movie . . . just getting to know each other . . . And I felt something." But like the professionals they are, they both agreed nothing should happen. So, like LJ and Peter, they made a "no dating" pact so that they could concentrate on set! But that spark is there, and thank goodness, because not only is a sequel coming soon, there's also a *TATBILB 3*!!

Great news, but it still leaves us with the burning question: Who was, and who IS, Noah dating? It might be easier to start with who is NOT dating Noah. Well, Lana. And since he kept himself off the radar for a while, we don't really know who he dated before he became the Internet's ★fake★ boyfriend. We know he dated Kelli Berglund from *Lab Rats* when he was younger. He *was* dating Angeline Appel from 2016 to 2018, whom you may have seen as Rachel in *Babysitter's Black Book*. Something they have in common is that they both were born in Miami. Something else they just might also have in common, unfortunately, is stubbornness, since we know that Noah is a Taurus and Angeline is a Leo. That can be a hard match. You've gotta take turns bending a little, you know?

Like a swirled SCOOP! Noah with Camila Cabello sent comments whirling when they met on the set of her video for "Havana."

He played the love interest, who at first seems "a young thug" with his slick suit and gold jewelry, but by the end is the sweet boy next door. Hmmm, sound familiar?? If they did date, though, it wasn't for long, because she's now the bona fide of Shawn Mendes.

And for a SCOOP! with sprinkles, there were rumors about Noah and Lily Collins after a flirty Instagram exchange and their hanging out at the 2019 *Vanity Fair* Oscars Party.

But we've not heard word of it again. Then, there was a little moment where we maybe thought something was going down with NC and Alexis Ren, according to an IGer who had seen them out. From there it was crickets. For a while! That chirping was soon replaced by more sightings of Noah and Alexis out dining and at airport pickups (!!). Those sightings escalated quickly . . . and we can now confirm that the two are, in fact, an item! In an interview, Alexis declared, "I love that man with all my heart." Squish!

Noah is not afraid to talk about love, dating, and relationships. At all. Like, really. So much so that we can pretty much get an idea of what Noah looks for in a bae—when he's looking, that is!

Noah isn't going to go all He-Man, pun intended, against rom-coms. He told *Teen Vogue*, "All I know is I like them. I'm really into love. I'm a hopeless romantic some days and a hopeful one on other days, so I hope to do more [rom-coms] moving forward."

Okay, so Netflix and chill. *Check.*

His Twitter posts are all the feels.

> Love deeply. Break your heart. Love deeper. Repeat.

> We don't love the way we want to be loved

> How long does it take to fall in Love? Depends how fast you jump.

He's got feels in his feels!

And Noah has the romantic-gesture thing down pat. He writes love notes (total Kavinsky move), and he once took a girlfriend back to the hometown she hadn't seen in years.

Are you tearing up yet???

Dude sounds fearless! But hol' up, hol' up. It goes deeper than that . . . The guy can simultaneously portray both the hot jock and the soulful dreamer. Check out what he says about that very human frailty we all have in some shape or another:

"I think we're all dealing with insecurity, and we hide that insecurity from the world, which, in turn, just hides us from the world. And it's only once we actually embrace these insecurities and love them that we can really love ourselves and others, fully."

So, let's embrace our insecurities because they are part of what makes us embraceable!

Can we hug it out?

But we need to get down to business—we still have to find out what NC looks for in a girl. Well, like we SCOOPed, he talks about it, and plenty! He told *E! News* that ideally it's "someone who takes care of themselves and someone honest" and NOT someone who doesn't "take care of themselves, like across the board, whether it is mentally, emotionally, hygiene or like just feeling good" or "shuts down and is passive-aggressive as opposed to someone who could communicate how they feel."

Sweet, we're getting there! So, he's no fan of

someone playing coy or not calling back because she got mad. And he's not into online hookups; he'd rather get to know a girl. "We are from a swipe-right generation, and that just comes to, *Oh you're cute, let's hook up*, and that's that. Where is actual, genuine connection that comes from spending quality time with someone?"

An example of quality time? We have a SCOOP! with a double dip! He was living at the W Hotel (welcome to the life of an actor), and they had a great rooftop pool, and the girl would come over around sunset.

Noah said, "Bring a book!" So they traded. He gave her *The Celestine Prophecy,* and she gave him *You Are the One* by Kute Blackson. And they read! For, like, three hours!

But, like most of us, Noah's familiar with heartbreak. That's okay, though—he's got himself covered. He's always 100 percent about his feels, and this subject's no different!

"I was in relationships when I didn't really know how to love myself fully, and it wasn't until I had my heart broken, and I was alone, and I learned to live with myself when I was alone, and to know the difference between being lonely and being alone, and it really taught me to find this authentic empowerment within myself."

This gives us a pretty good hint as to why Noah's able to enjoy being single, and how he's able to love himself fully—even after a tough breakup.

So, as you might have guessed, we're totally pulling for Noah and Alexis, but just in case, read on to catch our picks for why, where, what, and WHO would fit the bill for his perfect date in the future!

WHO SHOULD NOAH DATE?

Since we've given you so much SCOOP! about his thoughts on love, we're going all out with our best guesses on:

would be a great date for Noah Centineo.

Emma Watson

WHAT—A game of Quidditch

WHERE—A lovely English field somewhere in Yorkshire

WHY—Okay, so we all know Quidditch is physically impossible, but they could always toss the brooms and just do yoga on the lovely field. Did you know Emma is a certified yoga and meditation instructor? And she loves to read and writes in a journal. AND, he's read all the HP books and seen all the films. So. Much. In. Common!

Selena Gomez

WHAT—Sunset coffee

WHERE—Outdoor cafe with a view

WHY—He's admitted a crush on her and even said, "Selena Gomez seems like one of the coolest people ever. And she's an activist, as well."

Zendaya

WHAT—Romantic dinner

WHERE—NYC rooftop

WHY—NC says one of his skills is sneaking onto rooftops, and since we know she can fly from her work in *The Greatest Showman*, she'd be cool with the heights thing.

Laura Marano

WHAT—Piano-bar dinner

WHERE—Smoke Jazz & Supper Club

WHY—They go way back and know each other well, IRL, not online. She's an accomplished recording artist; he loves music and even plays guitar!

Kristine Froseth

WHAT—Beach picnic

WHERE—Malibu, naturally

WHY—We know it was fiction, but we felt bad for her character, Veronica, in *SBIAL*. Yes, she was a jerk at first and gave out Sierra's number, but she made a change and began to be kind. So, we feel her earlier behavior perhaps didn't warrant S not telling V her ex was out to manipulate her by making her feel stupid and then *posting the pic of their hookup on the scoreboard at a football game.* Really? Whoa, whoa, whoa! ·

Taylor Swift

WHAT—July Fourth (Taymerica!)

WHERE—Her house in Rhode Island

WHY—We're just kidding. He shouldn't go out with her.

Princess Sirivannavari Nariratana of Thailand

WHAT—A game of badminton

WHERE—Some beautiful grassy court in her country, Thailand

WHY—She's a professional badminton player, so she'd beat him, and he'd be impressed rather than embarrassed because he's so woke.

Elle Fanning

WHAT—Hiking

WHERE—Carmel, California

WHY—She told Scarlett Johansson for *Interview* magazine that when she and her friends go there, they always climb up the rocks and bust in on the golf course. Sounds right up Noah's alley. Plus, she looks kinda like Cameron Diaz, his first celeb crush.

Abigail Breslin

WHAT—Playing Pokémon Go

WHERE—Anywhere

WHY—They're both obsessed. He says it ruled his life for eight years, and she wants to make her house into a PokéStop. Now that's kismet!

Lily James

WHAT—Sunday brunch

WHERE—A cool London pub

WHY—We don't know, she just seems nice and cool, like Noah.

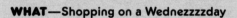

Liza Koshy

WHAT—Shopping on a Wednezzzzday

WHERE—The dollar store!

WHY—She could make him laugh for hours, and he'd love that!

Bella Hadid

WHAT—Romantic, candlelit dinner

WHERE—Paris

WHY—Noah could whisk her off her feet and give her all his great "how to get over someone" advice to recover from her inevitable breakup with The Weeknd.

CHAPTER 4

THE HIGH PRICE OF FAME

*Y*ou know how there are all these people these days famous just for being famous? Like, what skill, talent, or #*GOALS* have they truly achieved to deserve said fame? The Kardashians, kids of rich people (celebutante Olivia Jade, case in point), WAGs and HABs of just about any sports star, YouTubers, reality TV stars, Sasquatch . . . We could go on. And on. Really, what did Sasquatch ever do besides *serving looks* at tourists with nothing better to do than gawk at the Pacific Northwest woods for weeks on end?

Ummm. How did we get there?

Anyway, what we mean is that there is a massive difference between famous and famesque.

Noah is the former. We already gave you the

SCOOP! that he's been studying acting for a looonnng time, attending BAK Middle School of the Arts and auditioning for well over a decade. He has a craft. And he is famous for practicing that craft and practicing it well. His fame is earned.

You know the upside of fame. First, there's $pa-per$. Acting at Noah's level earns plenty of it. Then there's access. Dinner reservations, luxury vacations, and the velvet rope just drops. People want you around. Designers want you to wear their clothes. You saw his Calvin Klein ad, right? Fame creates opportunity, which creates more paper and more fame. Once it gets going, it's like a tornado.

And Noah has expressed gratitude. On *Jimmy Kimmel Live!* he announced, "I love your love."

But like any tornado, there's usually some damage.

We all know if you're famous, everybody's up in your grill. It's hard to make a move without everyone talking about it. It's like school times a billion.

So, get this: Noah appeared on *The Late Late*

Show with James Corden alongside Busy Philips, and the girl straight up OUTED him for ghosting one of her friends. Apparently they were chatting on a dating app, and Noah went crickets on her (turns out she was forty, so our main question is what is she doing chatting with a guy in his early twenties?!?!?!). Can you IMAGINE having your receipts broadcast on CBS, where anyone who flips on their remote can watch, and then it goes viral? EEK!!

Never mind that Ms. Philips felt terrible about it afterward. (Again, why is she friends with a fortysomething who creeps on twentysomethings?) Damage done. Trust us; he got dragged for it. Who doesn't make a mistake? Who doesn't chat on the phone a bit and then decide, "Nope," but you never met, so an official breakup text feels too extra? We're not saying true ghosting is okay, but our point here is that regular peeps might get a hairy eyeball in homeroom, but for the world to know? That reeks.

Then there were the haters who complained when he was cast in *Charlie's Angels.* One even posted, "WHY is Noah Centineo in this please where did he come from," Um, *Charlie's Angels* is a remake of a remake of a show from the '70s! Don't get us wrong, we are psyched for this fun film, but to act as if it's Shakespeare (for more SCOOP! on Shakespeare, go to page 45) and because he was in rom-coms he doesn't belong there? What is *that*?

It's tall poppy syndrome. Meaning, people want to cut down others who are more successful than they are. Certain, um, we'll be nice and say "less evolved humans" can't see someone shine without the need to throw shade on it. Noah is genuinely having a moment, so some feel the need to tear him down.

Example: Remember those chiseled abs in the CK ad? Right, so who wouldn't work out like crazy before that photo shoot? And once it was over, who wouldn't treat themselves to a cheat meal . . . or four? Sure, maybe Noah had a couple of extra scoops of rocky road and then posted a pic of the not-so-chiseled abs on Instagram, but who cares??? In the pic, Noah is holding a phone to his ear with the witty caption: "Mom I'll be home in May." Then he got body-shamed. Harshly. People said things like, "Jeesh he let himself go," and "Yikes what happened." So, everyone is susceptible to IG trolls, but Noah has over seventeen million followers. Can you even?

We can't. And get this:

SCOOP! is that everyone was stanning NC and Lana Condor so much that when they found out she had an IRL boyfriend, Anthony De La Torre, they started dissing him online.

Hateful things, like how she should be dating Noah instead. To the point where not only did Anthony have to disable his IG comments but he even had to go private for a while. Lana was rightfully confused. "If you say you support me, why would you hurt someone I love?" she asked.

So, clearly, once you become a household name, people feel free to use you as a digital punching bag.

Then there's the other side, where the love is a little too much. We're talking stalkers. Scary. Noah told Jimmy Kimmel about an incident where he flew into NYC and was at baggage claim when he felt some people watching him. He stepped to the side, took off his headphones, and saw four people who were just staring at him.

"I was like, 'Hi,' and they were like, 'Hey! Hi! How was your flight?' And I was like, 'It, it was good. How was yours?' And they were like, 'Oh, no, we didn't fly. We were here for you.'"

Uh-oh.

"They somehow knew I was flying into JFK and the time I was going there," he continued. "And they parked in the same place where the driver parks, and then they walked us to the car, and then they followed the car to the city."

His driver shook them off, but still, it goes from bad to worse.

"I went back a second time . . . to the same airport," Centineo explained. ". . . And they were there again. The same people, except they added another person."

They wanted to apologize for their previous creeping.

"I love the fact that you care about me . . . Just don't follow me. And the rest is cool, like—just don't follow me."

He's got major gratitude for his fans. But we think perhaps it's a bit uncomfy when people decide they have a right to invade a public figure's privacy.

He explained to *Vice* magazine: "I don't want to close myself off to people or opportunities. But I also have to learn how to protect myself."

There's a lesson here, which you already know, but we'll put it out there, anyway.

SUPPORT > STALKING

The price of fame is high, indeed. In Noah's case, it's literal. He had to hire a security guard to make sure nothing too spoopy happens!

HERE'S THE SCOOP!

ON SHAKESPEARE

Did you know that William Shakespeare popularized more than 1,700 words?

That's right! The Bard has done more to shape the English language than any other writer in history.

Here's a small sampling of some words Shakespeare popularized:

bedroom lonely zany moonbeam
torture eyeball elbow cold-blooded
gossip . . .

And the list goes on! We can thank Shakespeare for his generous★ contributions to the English language. Without him, it would be rather lackluster★!

 ★Tiny Scoop! He popularized these two words.

CHAPTER 5

TO TWEET OR NOT TO TWEET

We've all felt cute and might delete later. It's a natural human phenomenon to say or do something, then decide you want to take it back. We're all navigating the difference between an offhand comment reaching only the ear of your bestie and an off-brand comment reaching the ears of everyone online. Noah Centineo is in the same spot. Times seventeen million.

He handles it like a pro. His Twitter bio used to be one word, *feels*. Instagram is simply "Hi." Even though it doesn't seem to be on his feed any longer (hmmmm, why, we wonder?), *feels* sounds about right for a Taurus, the feeliest sign of them all and ruled by Venus. The soulful and searching posts are on brand with Peter or Jamey.

"I'm trying to discern whether or not 'feeling lost' is a cultural factor specialized to My Generation (z) or a biological rite of passage in the process of maturity. Or does every generation feel lost because we've made unwise choices for hundreds if not thousands of years?"

These are not the shares of a guy who goes through life without introspection and reflection.

In 2018, he wrote, "We were so good together . . . but doubt would always whisper in my ear when we were apart."

Ohhhhhhhh, who was *that* about?? Point is, he isn't afraid to put himself out there. You know how guys are supposed to be all tough, but when they put that above all else, it just leads to miscommunication and awkwardness? NC seems to know better.

Sometimes the tweets are silly but still truthful: "Pokémon owned my soul for like 8 solid years." We hear you! We love that he's not trying to be all cool, and he isn't afraid to make fun of himself.

Those are the kinds of people that are the funnest to be around. If you can't laugh at yourself, you can't laugh at much.

Then there are the posts that are a bit off-the-wall and artful. "Truth is hidden but it does not hide." That's true!

NC clearly believes in the truth, and he's not hiding anything. Like when some people began ragging on *SPF-18,* a film he made before *SBIAL* and *TATBILB.* To be fair, *SPF-18* is a bit confusing, and it was really hard to tell exactly how Keanu Reeves fit into the plot. Anyway, rather than defend the film or rag on it as well, all he said was, "I can't abandon the person I used to be so I carry him."

That, my friends, is first-rate diplomacy! And wise. Everybody goes through different phases, right? Justin Timberlake had "Do Your Thing" with ★NSync before going solo and dropping "Can't Stop the Feeling." Ben Affleck won Razzie Awards for bombs like *Gigli* and *Daredevil* before directing the Academy Award–winning *Argo*. Noah Centineo owns his less-than-stellar movies, too!

Noah's posts are definitely stellar, though. So much so that singer-songwriter Liz Bissonette made a song comprised only of his tweets. And it's actually a good song!

"A lot of his tweets are really poetic," Liz said. "The hardest part was picking which tweets to use, and figuring out how to help them flow and rhyme."

She's clearly impressed with his posts, but, of course, there's always the gloomers saying it's making fun of him. We've got the SCOOP! for them. NC beat them to it.

His response? "This is fantastic <3 thanks for trying to make me less of a cringe."

Always positive and smart. Speaking of smart,

Noah's posts are not confined to random thoughts and love poems. He cares about what's going on in the world and is totally woke. He shares his concerns about inequality, racism, injustice, and the environment on both Twitter and Instagram.

"Lemme get this straight. I can bring 1,000 water balloons to a public park in Beverly Hills with 6 of my friends and go crazy without a singular squad car . . .

But when a micro water balloon fight breaks out in Watts, we send helicopters and hella squad cars with rubber bullets."

And he retweeted, "Watch @KillerMike on @billmaher defend @BernieSanders's free college plan! 'As an American I don't mind investing in a greater America.' Trade school and higher education are investments in our people and our future."

Yes, there are always gloomers who find any way to say something negative, saying he cares too much. Huh? Is there such a thing? Wait, they're couching it in these terms: He's a thirst architect.

He posts flattering pictures of himself. *As you do.*

His are professional grade, though, like soft-focus shots of him lounging and reading without a shirt on. Or in a tree. Or posting a screenshot of his face after someone didn't pick up a FaceTime call, with the caption "Why y'all never pick up?"

As you do.

In his case, though, millions of followers responded that they would always pick up his calls. Critters (constant criticizers) are claiming that it's just too much, that he's always setting up a thirst trap. One blogger claims that "he is actively participating in his role as the object of our affections."

Hmmm. I get that. But isn't that what actors do? Isn't that part of the job?

For an interview with Allison P. Davis of *The Cut,* Noah met the writer at the New York Aquarium at Coney Island. She admits to setting it up as the perfect date. So who is calling whom an architect? It was a hot day with little to no AC, and he was such a kind, considerate gentleman trying to find a cooler spot to make the writer comfortable, that it made her *un*comfortable. "It's a specific sort of gallantry I recognize from his roles, the ones he describes as manly and masculine, but also 'sensitive, emotionally intelligent, loving, nurturing, and protective.'"

Why that makes her uncomfortable is beyond us! Sounds like he's a nice guy. Which she also admits!

"That's it. He's just fully nice and hot at a time that feels like 'nice and hot' is a rare resource. He's a throwback to a more classic sort of wish fulfillment."

Now, we sort of get why a girl would maybe second-guess being around such charm! He knows how to pour it on. And we'll admit that the "Dear Love" series on Instagram by photographer Sarah Bahbah was a bit extra.

But isn't being extra what acting is about? Last time we looked, an acting career depends on having lots of followers, being charming, and having people want to see you on screen. Noah Centineo is bringing all that and more.

Remember that tall poppy syndrome, and remember that everything the critters cut him down for is exactly what he should be doing. There's a reason Davis titled her piece "Noah Centineo, Shameless Heartthrob: My date with the best thirst architect the Internet's ever seen."

Rock on, NC! Nailed it!

Of course, we have a social media SCOOP! Noah and Lana Condor just posted an adorable video in which they announce not only the release date for *P.S. I Still Love You*, aka *TATBILB2* (February 12, 2020, just in time for Valentine's Day—no mistake there!) but that there will be a *TATBILB 3*! They just wrapped filming!

Noah Centineo is using social media exactly as it was meant to be used.

For a fun treat, next up we have a list of his funniest tweets!

NOAH'S FUNNIEST TWEETS

Where am I? What day is it? Why did I take a 3 hour nap at 6 pm?

Why is it . . . that something can be so unfunny that it's funny . . . but not so funny that it's unfunny?

If you have an opportunity to be in a room with Russell Brand. Please take it.

I ate salmon for dinner and now my burps taste like coffee ice cream. I'm kinda disgusted but like . . . also kinda stoked

Pokémon owned my soul for like 8 solid years

Your Venmo feed is the real tea

I wish tweeting that I'm overwhelmed would help me feel less overwhelmed.

bumping "your love" by the outfield in New York City has got to be one of my favorite activities of 2019

Dude . . . you know when you wake up after being asleep at the wheel for a few weeks? That's me right now

Yoooooooo somebody just destroyed one of the bathrooms on this plane and I'm not sure what needs to be done but an ejector seat is my next option.

Just spent the last hour and a half living vicariously through my Instagram fan accounts

Unfortunately I have absolutely no IPhone X's to giveaway. Which leads me to my next point, My instagram is Hacked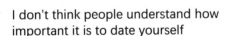

I don't think people understand how important it is to date yourself

I just yelled at myself for 3 minutes in the car because I was 15 minutes late to a meeting that I had at 10am. When I got there I realized the meeting is actually on Wednesday.

pre-sunrise ubers always end with me on Twitter.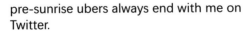

CHAPTER 6

GIVING BACK

We SCOOPed a bit of this in the last chapter, but we're going into a deep dive here. Noah Centineo is all about giving back, and he uses his following to get important messages out there. Consider this tweet from author Mark Z. Danielewski, who wrote this after spending an evening with Noah:

> "Great time last night talking about renewable energy, the prison industrial complex, and . . . lemon zest." @noahcent

We're not sure what the lemon zest is about, but the rest is clear. Noah is WOKE. An essential part of his wokeness, and one we particularly admire, is that Noah isn't about going out and partying.

Because how can someone be woke about anything, really, if they're in an altered reality? They can't. And they stay at the mental level where they started altering that reality. Put it this way: heavy partying isn't interesting. It's a bore. Noah is anything but boring—he quit drinking and stays completely sober. And he's all the more alive and awake to the world around him for doing so.

NC isn't wasting a moment. It's a good thing, too, because there's not much time to waste. The world needs to make some changes, and it will be up to Gens XYZ to usher them in. Noah is taking the lead!

He's not afraid to tackle tough issues, and here are some of the main ones:

He's done charity work for the Watts Empowerment Center in Los Angeles. They pair youth from the Watts Housing Projects with successful professionals to help them realize their potential. So obvs, EQUALITY matters to NC.

He champions not only economic equality but

also gender equality! He speaks to girl power, and told *Vice* magazine that "[Men] weren't just born misogynists! We were *taught* these ethics and morals." He says, "And it *is* a gender thing because clearly one gender has been intimately oppressed for far longer than the other. It's about time that we step up and have reverence and respect for one another."

Those tweets, plus the fact that he was up all night with a friend discussing the prison industrial complex mean that INJUSTICE is on his mind, too.

He retweeted this post: "Looking at how they casually arrest a white killer who just killed 19+ americans in El Paso vs how they treat/killed Eric Garner, am [sic] unarmed black man for 'selling cigarettes' tells you everything you need to know about the current state of America!"

This is a dude who not only thinks about the welfare of others, but he gets involved. We think the fact that he does, and that he lets it show, is a huge part of his appeal. Thirst architecture or not! We'll take a guy who cares over a guy playing it cool any day!

Speaking of cool, NC made a brave speech about ANTI-BULLYING while accepting the 2019 Teen Choice Award for best comedy movie actor. He is all about the underdog!

"You know, I really just want to honor all of the kids out there that are being bullied and that have it hard and come from a really messed-up situation. I just love you guys, and you cannot let anybody tell you you cannot do something. You can't. If I am from South Florida and I made it here, you can, too."

He doesn't stop there. EDUCATION is in his sights, too. He retweeted the following post from NowThis:

"This school sends students to yoga class instead of detention, and the results are incredible."

Yaaaasssss! The educational system could use a lot more mindfulness and yoga. And hey, guys, while we're at it, that whole thing where you take a kid's recess if they don't finish their work? Can we toss that? Because humans need to move around. A lot. It's a "use it or lose it" thing. It's SELF-CARE. Which Noah talks about as well.

He advises to meditate, do yoga, unplug, and go wander outside! It's crucial to well-being.

"Put your phone down, and go outside and walk around, or read for 10 minutes or do something not on your phone intentionally for a second where it

HERE'S THE SCOOP! ON YOGA:

Did you know that yoga is speculated to be first practiced as early as 3000 BCE?

Here are some other notable inventions, discoveries, and introductions from the third millennium BCE:

- The potter's wheel is invented in Mesopotamia.
- The Egyptians discover the use of papyrus for writing.
- The Great Pyramid of Giza is built.

During this time, the world population was sixty million. In 2020, the world population is projected to be 7.58 billion people.

forces you to engage with the outside world, it's very therapeutic and invigorating!"

We know the ENVIRONMENT is also high on Noah's list. Totally makes sense. What he's said about enjoying the outdoors, hiking, swimming? He means it! His posts often ask his fellow humans to keep our planet beautiful and a viable place to live. Noah even went so far as to post a video of a livid Bill Nye explaining that if we don't stop our current destruction of natural resources, the Earth will go down in flames. It's a funny video, but, sadly, it's also true!

Here's another baller retweet from @PrisonReformMvt, who originally posted a video of someone filling up an empty plastic bottle from the tap of a prison in Mississippi. The water, coming straight from the faucet, was dirt brown. Here's the text that accompanied the video:

"This is tap water from the faucets at Parchman State Prison in Mississippi. The men say it smells like sewer- this is what they are forced to bathe in and drink . . ."

W magazine noticed Noah's activism and asked him if he is hoping to use his platform to help address a bunch of social issues. Noah is on it:

"Absolutely. I'm currently strategizing the best way for me to leverage my platform, my growing platform, my friends' platforms, to help fight a various group of social injustices. Currently, I'm not really able to discuss it because it's still in the developing process, but to answer your question, absolutely."

We are chomping at the bit to see what he's planning!

In the meantime, we are psyched to SCOOP! that he paired up with Omaze to auction off a date for charity— a picnic and sunset hike, natch!

He raised money for two causes. One, his mother's charity that donates resources to children in Nairobi, called Project Kazuri. Two, his best friend's charity, The Guthy-Jackson Charitable

Foundation, which funds research to cure neuro-myelitis optica, an autoimmune disease. Both are super-worthy causes.

NC and his mom made a hilarious video to announce the campaign. She said he would keep the winner safe on the hike but had a warning, too:

"Don't bring pets, because he'll play with your pet, and you will be all by yourself the entire time."

Anyone who loves animals is good in our book! Another sign that he's a good guy is that fab relationship with his mom. They look like they have a blast together, and she obviously raised him right!

NC also teased an upcoming project on both Instagram and Twitter, pointing the lens at his baseball cap that said "10 Tanker Air Carrier–Aerial Firefighting," and zoomed in on a massive plane. Noah is clearly interested in helping to put out the Amazon wildfires. That's dedication!

Noah has even said at one point that before he hit it big, he was thinking of going to a third-world country to dedicate his life to charity. Luckily, he did hit it big and is finding ways to give back just as much.

It's always nice to see a celebrity use their platform to make the world a better place.

CHAPTER 7

WHAT'S NEXT?

So, we've given you the SCOOP! on every-thing Noah has been up to recently. He's been a tour de force!

The SCOOP! with a cherry on top is that not only is there a release date for *To All the Boys: P.S. I Still Love You*, but that the squad just finished filming *TATBILB 3*.

As ever, Noah was grateful and put it out there via Twitter!

"Tonight was my last night as Peter Kavinsky.

I hope you all love these last installments as much as we do. Forever grateful for the opportunity to be yours

Thank you Lana, thank you Michael,
Thank you Matt, Thank you Netflix,
grateful to every person who told this
story with us"

If the fact that there won't be more than three *TATBILB* films bums you out as much as it does us, take heart!

Even if he's not playing PK, Noah is still pouring on the charm, and we'll be getting plenty of it.

Flip side to excelling as the perfect boyfriend in the rom-coms is that it's easy to get typecast. It happens to actors. Scads. Can you picture Will Smith as anything but a hilarious cop? Or Keira Knightley as anything but a smart but stifled lady from a previous century? How about Jim Carrey as anything but the eccentric crazy guy? If someone is good at pulling our heartstrings, they often keep getting cast as the romantic lead.

Well, we've got another SCOOP! for you. Noah is not playing the super stud BF in his next film but a charming geek opposite Kristen Stewart and Elizabeth Banks in *Charlie's Angels*.

Do we hear right? A geek!?!

Yep. Even though Noah was superb as the hot dude in previous films, he always portrayed his characters soulfully. He may have been the star football or lacrosse player, but he was vulnerable and sensitive. We can totally see him geeking out. But still cute!

Stepping wayyyyy back from being the Internet's boyfriend, Noah will also appear in a film directed by Jackie Chan, set in 1930s Shanghai and Europe. There's definitely no suburban PK or Brooks Rattigan in that scenario. It's called *The Diary* and costars Kevin Kline. Not much is out there about the exact deets, but we do know from IMDb.com that in it, a "young man leaves Shanghai to come to Europe and reunite with the love of his life."

This is great news because even Noah himself was worried about being stuck playing the "fake boyfriend." He hopes to keep branching out and challenging himself. "Everything that I'm doing right now, everything that I have done or everything I have lined up are stepping stones. I'm not anywhere near where I want to be," is how he put it to *The Hollywood Reporter.*

Noah will also star as He-Man in *Masters of the Universe*, which is set to release in 2021. "It's a really big responsibility," Noah said. "It's a new universe and it's a new studio and their take on a universe."

He told MTV News that he has already been busy practicing the character's "I have the power!" battle cry. "I've been screaming it until my voice is vocally fried, man." In the interview, you can also see that he's been at the gym, and often he's crazy buffed up!

"It's a big opportunity and I feel more than ready to tackle it."

As we described, Noah keeps it at 100 percent, and playing He-Man is no different. You know he is up for the challenge!

Next up: like a multi-SCOOP! sundae, we're compiling a listicle of characters—funny, smart, soulful, crazy, and more—who we think would be fun to see Noah play in the future. And feel free to jump ahead to page 92 to write your own ideas on who you would like to see Noah play on-screen!

SCOOP! EXTRA

NOAH'S PROPHECY

Characters we can see Noah Centineo playing in the future & the improv moves he would give each one:

NOAH CALHOUN
from *The Notebook*—
Tweets about his heartbreak when Allie marries Lon

JACK DAWSON
from *Titanic*—
Back-pocket spin on the ship's bow

INDIANA JONES
from all the IJ movies—
In addition to fighting spectacularly against the Third Reich, he launches a full media campaign against their violations of human rights

TROY BOLTON
from *High School Musical*—
Can't help but throw in a couple of flosses when he's auditioning for a laugh

GUS WATERS from *The Fault in Our Stars*—Gives Hazel *The Celestine Prophecy* instead of a book about a video game

JAMES BOND from Too Many Films to Name Here—Drinks kombucha instead of martinis

EDWARD CULLEN from *Twilight*—Instead of warning Bella that she "really should stay away from me," he says, "Whoa, whoa, whoa!"

MR. DARCY from *Pride and Prejudice*—Still goes swimming in his shirt but takes an underwater pic

BATMAN from Yet Again Too Many Films to Name—Moves a bowl of popcorn out of the way before slamming the villain

HAN SOLO from Star Wars—Sits down with Darth Vader for a heart-to-heart because he's not cool with battling him before first giving him a chance to redeem himself

ROCKY BALBOA from *Rocky II*—Looks better than Sylvester Stallone running up those steps but trips and laughs hysterically as all those kids pile onto him

JAKE RYAN from *Sixteen Candles*—Wouldn't break up with his popular, drunk girlfriend by handing her over to the geek (so not okay); would wait until she's sober and kindly tell her they aren't right for each other

CHARLIE CHAPLIN in *The Tramp*—Doesn't change a thing because he connects so deeply with the often heartbroken, always funny character

73

CHAPTER 8

THE TAKEAWAY

So, our main SCOOP! on Noah Centineo? It's not that he's talented, or that he keeps it 100 percent to hone his acting chops, or that he deserves his fame, or that he's branching out into films other than rom-coms. Nor is about whom he's dating or if he's a thirst architect.

> **Our main takeaway is that this is a nice person. And even though he is all those other things that we just listed, being a kind human being seems the most important attribute.**

He treats people well. He stays sober to make *sure* he can treat people well.

Have you ever read anything about him being a jerk? We haven't. And we all know celebs can't make a move these days without a privacy leak. Like when Busy Philips chattered about Noah ghosting her friend. But given the circumstances of that ghosting, we're not sure it translates into NC being out of line, and we have to wonder if Busy Philips's friend wasn't the catfisher Noah talked about to *Teen Vogue*.

"It happened a year and a half ago," he said. "I met someone on Instagram and I developed an ostensibly intimate relationship with them and it turns out they weren't who they were."

You know our stance on that—he probably realized she was old enough to be his mom and slowly . . . backed . . . away . . .

Speaking of moms, Noah has also said he calls his mom all the time for advice. That's so solid. Last time we looked, guys aren't usually ringing up their mom on a daily basis. And from that Omaze video they made, you can tell they have a great time together. She even says you'd have a lot of fun around him. We know, we know, is there a mom on Earth who would say their son isn't nice? Probably not, but there would've been other hints. Plus, she says he'd keep you safe on a hike. Chivalry is not dead!

Just the fact that he's making the video and going on a sunset hike with someone he doesn't know in order to raise money for charity is a clue right there.

Plus, Mrs. C. said if you brought your pet on the hike, he'd probably play with it the whole time. Animal people? Always good in our books.

Noah himself asks you to join him "in petting every single puppy on the hike." He even kind of bounces around like a puppy, with an infectious smile that seems completely genuine. If it's not, he should get an Oscar just for that!

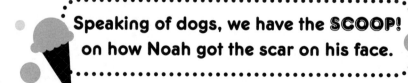

Speaking of dogs, we have the SCOOP! on how Noah got the scar on his face.

"I got attacked when I was six years old by a mastiff," he said. "He ripped a hole in my face, so you could see my teeth, my gums, and all the way through my tongue to the other side. There was a massive, gaping hole."

You know what's interesting? He forgave the dog. Right away.

"I specifically remember him lunging, being pulled away from him, and then looking back and seeing him cock his head like he didn't really understand what happened. Some people were like, 'Do you wanna put the dog down?' I was crying, like, 'No, he didn't mean to do it!'"

Even more interesting, he said that six weeks later, his family got a puppy. SUCH a smart move. His parents made sure that one bad experience didn't color his whole vision of dogs, which is often the case if someone has an early bad experience. So, Noah learned right away that while some dogs might be aggressive, most aren't. That applies to everything in life. It's the one-bad-apple thing.

It doesn't spoil the whole bunch.

"Getting a dog, a bigger dog, after that was great," he said. "And now, the bigger the dog, the better."

Like we SCOOPed, it's all in the family. Noah's father, Greg Centineo, has said, "I knew once Noah got a platform of awareness and the world had a chance to witness what we have all witnessed for twenty-two years of his life, the world would love him, too."

Clearly, the world does indeed love Noah Centineo and not just because he's hot. You know how the people that you're around every day know the real you? Well, anyone and everyone who's worked with Noah pretty much adores him, too. Here are the greatest hits:

His *The Fosters* family thinks he's the best! They posted a picture of him with the caption, "To the boy we've always loved."

Laura Marano, who he worked with on both *Austin & Ally* and *The Perfect Date*, said: "He's so lovely. And he really hasn't changed his loveliness and nice personality since he was 15."

Sierra Burgess Is a Loser costar Shannon Purser: "Noah was just like genuinely kind and lovable from day one."

Last but not least, there's the *TATBILB* squad:

Anna Cathcart loved being around Noah and Lana, saying "Lana and Noah . . . they're so comfortable with each other and best friends, so it was awesome being with all three of us."

Janel Parrish told *HollyWire* that Noah "is so charming and amazing."

Lana? Well, they're the best of friends. When they won for Best Kiss on the 2019 MTV Movie & TV Awards, Lana said, "I just wanted to say thank you to Noah for being an amazing partner."

And after they wrapped on *TATBILB 3*, she tweeted, "You'll always be my Peter K. & I'll always be your Lara Jean, that I can promise you." Squish!

Even the journalist who called him a "thirst architect" conceded that he was nice! Not perfect, but pretty great.

Do you know what we would love to leave you with? One of the nicest SCOOPs ever. A journalist asked him if there is anything he would never post. His answer? It's gold:

"I mean, yeah, sure. I don't think I would ever shame someone."

It's so easy to jump on the bandwagon of calling someone out publicly for mistakes or even bad behavior. While we don't condone any bad behavior and are totally on board with doing anything and everything in our power to make sure things are fair and right, the jump to "cancel" people seems unkind, too. So, do us a favor, and if someone is doing something wrong, either DM them or, if you know them, have a heart-to-heart.

If someone has done something off or wrong, before you click, remember these words made famous by Jamey/Brooks/Peter/Noah:

"Whoa, whoa, whoa."

Because we're betting you're not ready to say BFN yet, we have a huge treat.

Since you know Noah so well based on all our SCOOPs, take this quiz on how he would react to situations IRL.

Good luck!

THE ULTIMATE
NOAH CENTINEO QUIZ

How well do you know Noah based on everything we've SCOOPed?

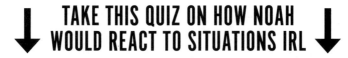

1. Lana Condor texts Noah that she's lost her car keys, and he's an hour away on set. What does he do?

  A. CALLS AAA FOR HER
  B. SENDS HER AN UBER
  C. POSTS HER TEXTS ON INSTAGRAM
     WITH A LAUGHING EMOJI
  D. DROPS EVERYTHING AND HAULS IT
     TO WHERE SHE IS TO MAKE SURE SHE
     GETS IN HER CAR AND HOME OKAY

2. His best friend gets dumped by text. Noah does what?

A. TAKES HIM OUT TO A CLUB

B. TAKES HIM ON A HIKE AND TALKS ABOUT LIFE

C. SETS HIM UP WITH ANOTHER GIRL ASAP

D. SHAMES THE GIRL ONLINE

3. He falls in love. Fast and deeply. How does he handle it?

A. GETS SO OVERWHELMED HE GHOSTS HER

B. KEEPS DATING AROUND JUST IN CASE SHE DUMPS HIM

C. TRIES TO COMMUNICATE OPENLY; TAKES HER ON FUN, ACTIVE DATES; EXPRESSES HIS GRATITUDE FOR FINDING HER

D. ASKS HER TO MARRY HIM ON THE FIRST DATE

4. Road trip with his family! Does he . . .

A. INSIST ON DRIVING

B. INSIST ON NAVIGATING AND GETS EVERYONE LOST

C. BRING HIS BEST FRIEND, AND THEY ROCK OUT IN THE BACK SEAT

D. STARE AT HIS PHONE THE WHOLE TIME

5. He's on a first date, and the girl gets some sad news about a friend. What does Noah do?

A. OFFERS TO DRIVE THEM BOTH TO HER FRIEND'S HOUSE AND SEE WHAT THEY CAN DO TO HELP

B. GRABS HER PHONE AND CALLS THE FRIEND TO SEE IF HIS DATE CAN CALL HER LATER

C. GETS ANNOYED THAT SHE LOOKED AT HER PHONE

D. SUGGESTS TO HIS DATE THAT SHE LET HER FRIEND DEAL ON HER OWN

6. Noah has a night to himself. Does he . . .

A. HEAD OUT TO A COFFEEHOUSE AND READ

B. TEXT HIS FRIENDS TO SEE IF THEY WANT TO HANG OUT AND GO GRAB A HEALTHY DINNER

C. MEDITATE AND DO SOME DOWNWARD DOGS

D. ALL OF THE ABOVE

7. He finds out someone is catfishing him. What does he do?

A. GHOSTS HER

B. TWEETS HER NUMBER AND OUTS HER

C. DMS OR CALLS TO SAY, "THAT'S TOTALLY NOT COOL, AND PLEASE DON'T DO IT TO ANYONE ELSE," BECAUSE HE LEARNED A LESSON FROM THE SITUATION WITH BUSY PHILIPS'S FRIEND

D. GOES OUT WITH HER ANYWAY, BECAUSE SHE'S CUTE

8. He forgets to eat lunch, and he's starving, so he . . .

A. DRIVES THROUGH IN-N-OUT BURGER

B. TWISTS OPEN AN AVOCADO AND EATS IT RIGHT FROM THE SKIN

C. MAKES SOMEONE ON SET ORDER HIM PIZZA

D. SKIPS THE MEAL ALTOGETHER; HE ISN'T VERY HEALTH CONSCIOUS

9. He's late to meet a crush, and it's the third time he's been late, so he . . .

A. DOESN'T CALL TO APOLOGIZE AND LET HER KNOW; SHE CAN WAIT

B. GASLIGHTS HER AND PRETENDS THEY WERE SUPPOSED TO MEET LATER

C. DECIDES THAT SINCE SHE'LL BE UPSET, HE DOESN'T WANT TO DEAL; DECIDES TO NO-SHOW

D. NONE OF THESE, BECAUSE HE'S NOT A SOCIOPATH

10. He's walking down the street and runs into an excited dog that jumps all over him. Noah . . .

A. IS SO EXCITED TO PLAY WITH THE DOG THAT HE MAKES HIMSELF LATE TO SET (BUT CALLS TO APOLOGIZE)

B. FREAKS OUT BECAUSE HE'S AFRAID OF DOGS

C. TELLS THE OWNER THEY SHOULD CONTROL THE DOG

D. ASKS THE OWNER TO PAY FOR HIS DRY CLEANING SINCE THE DOG MUDDIED HIS CLOTHES

WRITE YOUR OWN SCOOP!

What are your three favorite roles Noah has played? Why?

1 _____

_____

_____

2 _____

_____

_____

3 _____

_____

_____

Noah is passionate about helping to save the Amazon rain forest from deforestation. What are some causes you are passionate about?

1 _____

_____

_____

2 _____

_____

_____

3 _____

_____

_____

Who are some actors and actresses you'd like to see Noah share the screen with?

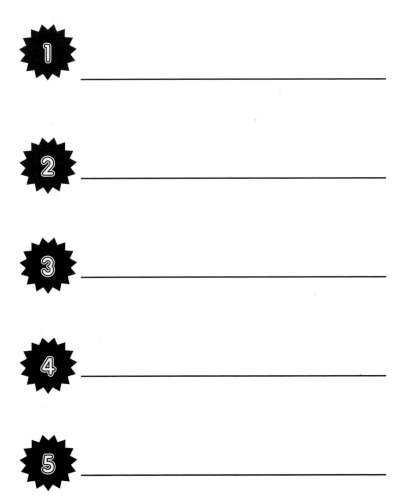

1 _____

2 _____

3 _____

4 _____

5 _____

Noah will star as He-Man in *Masters of the Universe* in 2021. What are some other franchise characters you would like to see Noah play in the future? Why?

1 _____

_____

_____

2 _____

_____

_____

3 _____

_____

_____

_____

Noah writes some pretty funny tweets on his Twitter account. What are some of your favorites?

1
_____

_____

_____

_____

2
_____

_____

_____

_____

3
_____

_____

_____

_____

ANSWER KEY

QUIZ: DO YOU KNOW YOUR LINES? (PAGE 11)
1. B, 2. C, 3. C, 4. D, 5. A, 6. B, 7. D, 8. A

THE ULTIMATE NOAH CENTINEO QUIZ (PAGE 83)
1. D, 2. B, 3. C, 4. C, 5. A, 6. D, 7. C, 8. B, 9. D, 10. A

HELP US PICK THE
NEXT ISSUE OF

HERE'S HOW TO VOTE:

Go to

www.ReadScoop.com

to cast your vote for
who we should
SCOOP! next.